A-Z SUPER SC/ GREAT BRITAIN NORTHERN IRELAND

Journey Route Planning maps

Britain & Northern Ireland Road maps

Detailed Main Route maps

City and Town centre maps

Plans of 70 principal cities and towns in Britain

Sea Port & Channel Tunnel plans

Airport plans

Over 32,000 Index References

A	
Abbas Combe. *Som*	.4C 22
Abberley. *Worc*	.4B 60
Abberley Common. *Worc*	.4B 60
Abberton. *Essx*	.4D 54
Abberton. *Worc*	.5D 61
Abberwick. *Nmbd*	.3F 121
Abbess Roding. *Essx*	.4F 53
Abbey. *Devn*	.1E 13

Aberkenfig. *B'end* ....

Aberlady. *E Lot* ....

Aberlemno. *Ang* ....

Aberllefenni. *Gwyn* ....

Abermaw. *Gwyn* ....

Abermeurig. *Cdgn* ....

Aber-miwl. *Powy* ....

Abermule. *Powy* ....

Abernant. *Carm* ....

Abernant. *Rhon* ....

Including cities, towns, villages, hamlets and locations..........206 - 238

Index to Places of Interest

J	
Jackfield Tile Mus. (TF8 7ND)	..5A 72
Jane Austen's House Mus. (GU34 1SD)	.3F 25
Jarlshof Prehistoric & Norse Settlement (ZE3 9JN)	.10E 173
Jedburgh Abbey (TD8 6JQ)	.3A 120
Jervaulx Abbey (HG4 4PH)	.1D 98
JM Barrie's Birthplace (DD8 4BX)	.3C 144

Full postcodes to easily locate popular places of interest on your SatNav ....239 - 242

Motorway Junctions

Junction		M1	
2	Northbound	No exit, access from A1 only	
	Southbound	No access, exit to A1 only	
4	Northbound	No exit, access from A41 only	
	Southbound	No access, exit to A41 only	
6a	Northbound	No exit, access from M25 only	
	Southbound	No access, exit to M25 only	

Details of motorway junctions with limited interchange..................243

Safety Camera Information

Details of Safety Camera symbols used on the maps, and the responsible use of Camera information ....Inside back cover

---

EDITION 29 2020

Copyright © Geographers' A-Z Map Company Ltd.

www./az.co.uk

Contains OS data © Crown copyright and database rights 2019

Northern Ireland: This is Based upon Crown Copyright and is reproduced with the permission of Land & Property Services under delegated authority from the Controller of Her Majesty's Stationery Office, © Crown copyright and database right 2019 PMLPA No 100508. The inclusion of parts or all of the Republic of Ireland is by permission of the Government of Ireland who retain copyright in the data used. © Ordnance Survey Ireland and Government of Ireland.

Land & Property Services
Paper Map Licensed Partner
OS

This is a registered Trade Mark of Department of Finance and Personnel.

Safety Camera & Fuel Station Databases copyright 2019, © PocketGPSWorld.com. PocketGPSWorld.com's CamerAlert is a self-contained speed and red light camera warning system for SatNavs and Android or Apple iOS smartphones or tablets. Visit www.cameralert.com to download.

Base Relief by Geo-Innovations, © www.geoinnovations.co.uk

The Shopmobility logo is a registered symbol of The National Federation of Shopmobility

The representation on the maps of a road, track or footpath is no evidence of the existence of a right of way.

REFERENCE

MOTORWAY WITH NUMBER	M4 — s — Service Area
MOTORWAY (Under Construction / Proposed)	
MOTORWAY JUNCTIONS	5 — 7 Limited
PRIMARY ROUTE	A5
A ROAD	A272
NATIONAL BOUNDARY	
TOWNS SHOWN IN THE MILEAGE CHART	NORWICH

SCALE

0   10   20   30 Miles
0   10   20   30   40 Kilometres

IV

UNST
YELL
FETLAR
SHETLAND ISLANDS
WHALSAY
FOULA
Scalloway
Lerwick
BRESSAY
Sumburgh

FAIR ISLE

WESTRAY
EDAY
SANDAY
ROUSAY
STRONSAY
SHAPINSAY
Stromness
Kirkwall
ORKNEY ISLANDS
HOY
SOUTH RONALDSAY
John o'Groats
Thurso
A836
A99
A882

A968
A970
A971
A970
A971
A970
A970
A967
A966
A965
A964
A960
A961

ISLE OF LEWIS (EILEAN LEODHAIS)
Stornoway (Steòrnabhagh)
A857
A858
A858
A859
Tarbert (Tairbeart)
A859
HARRIS (NA HEARADH)
Leverburgh (An t-Ob)
Lochmaddy (Loch nam Madadh)
A865
A867
NORTH UIST (UIBHIST A TUATH)
BENBECULA (BEINN NA FAOGHLA)
A865
Uig
A855
A87
A850
Dunvegan
Portree
RAASAY
SOUTH UIST (UIBHIST A DEAS)
ISLE OF SKYE
A863
A865
Lochboisdale (Loch Baghasdail)
BARRA (BARRAIGH)
CANNA
A851
Castlebay (Bàgh a' Chaisteil)
RÙM
Mallaig
EIGG
MUCK
Kilchoan
Acharacle
COLL
Tobermory
A848
Lochaline
A849
ISLE OF MULL
TIREE
IONA
A849

OUTER HEBRIDES
INNER HEBRIDES

COLONSAY
JURA
A846
A846
A847
ISLAY
Tayinloan
A846
Port Ellen
GIGHA
Campbeltown

Portstewart
Portrush
Ballycastle
A2
A29
Coleraine
A2
A37
A44
A2
Letterkenny
N56
N13
N14
Londonderry
A6
A37
A29
A26
A43
A42
A2
NORTHERN
A54
A31
Strabane
N15
A5
A6
Ballymena
A42
Larne
A36
A57
A8
N56
Ardara
N15
A505
A6
Antrim
M2
M22
IRELAND
Crumlin
A52
Donegal
A5
A505
Lough Neagh
M2
A20
Ballyshannon
N15
A32
Omagh
A4
Dungannon
M1
BELFAST
A2
Strangford Lough
N16
A47
A46
A4
M12
A29
A1
A24
Enniskillen
A4
A28
Armagh
A1
Downpatrick
N59
A4
N16
A28
A25
Sligo
N59
Monaghan
N2

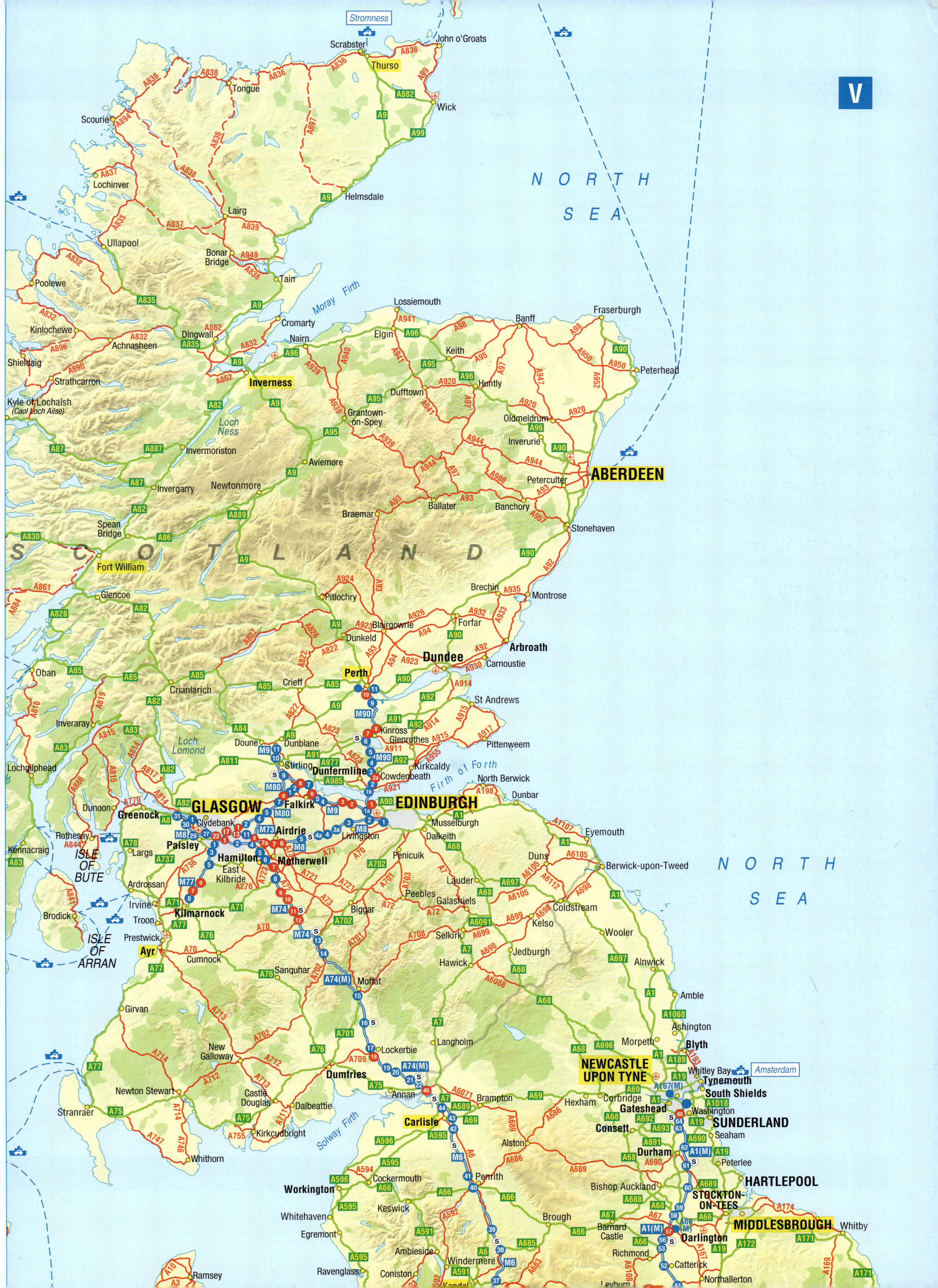

V
Stromness
Scrabster
Thurso
John o'Groats
Wick
Tongue
Scourie
Lochinver
Helmsdale
NORTH SEA
Lairg
Ullapool
Bonar Bridge
Tain
Poolewe
Moray Firth
Lossiemouth
Cromarty
Kinlochewe
Achnasheen
Dingwall
Nairn
Elgin
Banff
Fraserburgh
Shieldaig
Keith
Peterhead
Strathcarron
Inverness
Dufftown
Huntly
Kyle of Lochalsh
(Caol Loch Ailse)
Grantown-on-Spey
Oldmeldrum
Loch Ness
Inverurie
Invermoriston
Aviemore
Peterculter
ABERDEEN
Invergarry
Newtonmore
Ballater
Banchory
Braemar
Spean Bridge
Stonehaven
SCOTLAND
Fort William
Brechin
Montrose
Glencoe
Pitlochry
Forfar
Blairgowrie
Dunkeld
Arbroath
Dundee
Carnoustie
Oban
Crieff
Perth
Crianlarich
St Andrews
Inveraray
Kinross
Glenrothes
Pittenweem
Loch Lomond
Doune
Dunblane
Stirling
Kirkcaldy
Lochgilphead
Dunfermline
Cowdenbeath
Firth of Forth
North Berwick
Dunbar
Dunoon
Greenock
GLASGOW
Falkirk
EDINBURGH
Musselburgh
Clydebank
Airdrie
Livingston
Eyemouth
Rothesay
Kennacraig
ISLE OF BUTE
Paisley
Largs
Dalkeith
Hamilton
Motherwell
Penicuik
Duns
Berwick-upon-Tweed
NORTH SEA
East Kilbride
Lauder
Ardrossan
Peebles
Galashiels
Coldstream
Irvine
Kilmarnock
Biggar
Kelso
Brodick
Troon
Selkirk
Wooler
ISLE OF ARRAN
Prestwick
Ayr
Jedburgh
Cumnock
Hawick
Alnwick
Sanquhar
Moffat
Amble
Girvan
Ashington
Morpeth
Blyth
Lockerbie
Langholm
New Galloway
NEWCASTLE UPON TYNE
Whitley Bay
Amsterdam
Tynemouth
Dumfries
South Shields
Newton Stewart
Annan
Brampton
Hexham
Corbridge
Gateshead
Stranraer
Castle Douglas
Dalbeattie
Carlisle
Washington
SUNDERLAND
Consett
Seaham
Kirkcudbright
Solway Firth
Alston
Durham
Whithorn
Peterlee
Cockermouth
Penrith
HARTLEPOOL
Workington
Bishop Auckland
STOCKTON-ON-TEES
Keswick
Whitehaven
Brough
MIDDLESBROUGH
Egremont
Barnard Castle
Darlington
Whitby
Ambleside
Richmond
Windermere
Ramsey
Ravenglass
Coniston
Catterick
Northallerton
Kendal
Leyburn

Mileage Chart and Journey Times

This chart shows the distance in miles and journey time between two cities or towns in Great Britain. Each route has been calculated using a combination of motorways, primary routes and other major roads. This is normally the quickest, though not always the shortest route.

Average journey times are calculated whilst driving at the maximum speed limit. These times are approximate and do not include traffic congestion or convenience breaks.

To find the distance and journey time between two cities or towns, follow a horizontal line and vertical column until they meet each other.

For example, the 285 mile journey from London to Penzance is approximately 4 hours and 59 minutes.

Northern Ireland

Journey times

	Armagh	Coleraine	Enniskillen	Londonderry	Newry	Omagh	Belfast
Antrim	1:01	0:53	1:41	1:14	1:07	1:13	0:30
Armagh		1:32	1:06	1:39	0:31	0:46	0:57
Coleraine			2:09	0:52	2:00	1:43	1:11
Enniskillen				1:29	1:37	0:39	1:38
Londonderry					2:09	0:54	1:33
Newry						1:15	0:51
Omagh							1:16

Distance in miles

	Antrim	Armagh	Coleraine	Enniskillen	Londonderry	Newry	Omagh
Armagh	43						
Coleraine	40	61					
Enniskillen	86	49	94				
Londonderry	55	69	31	60			
Newry	53	19	92	69	88		
Omagh	54	35	65	27	34	54	
Belfast	22	41	56	84	72	37	68

Belfast to London = 440m / 9:46h (excluding ferry)
Belfast to Glasgow = 104m / 4:46h (excluding ferry)

Britain

Journey times

	Aberystwyth	Ayr	Birmingham	Bradford	Brighton	Bristol	Cambridge	Cardiff	Carlisle	Coventry	Derby	Doncaster	Dover	Edinburgh	Exeter	Fort William	Glasgow	Gloucester	Harwich	Holyhead	Inverness	Ipswich	Kendal	Kingston upon Hull	Leeds	Leicester	Lincoln	Liverpool	Manchester	Middlesbrough	Newcastle upon Tyne	Norwich	Nottingham	Oxford	Penzance	Perth	Plymouth	Portsmouth	Reading	Salisbury	Sheffield	Shrewsbury	Southampton	Southend-on-Sea	Stoke-on-Trent	Swansea	Thurso	Worcester	York	London
Aberdeen	8:21	3:31	7:13	6:28	9:56	8:26	8:15	8:55	4:08	7:27	7:09	6:25	10:16	2:39	9:38	3:38	2:50	7:55	9:32	7:41	2:30	9:08	4:55	6:51	6:16	7:40	7:07	6:13	6:01	5:16	4:39	9:18	7:14	8:18	11:22	1:48	10:16	9:33	8:57	9:21	6:42	7:07	9:25	9:22	6:28	9:31	4:52	7:35	6:07	9:03
Aberystwyth		6:34	2:34	3:27	5:21	2:44	4:00	2:29	4:24	2:52	2:56	3:45	5:41	6:20	3:51	8:13	5:53	2:34	5:17	2:29	8:39	4:53	3:40	4:20	3:29	3:18	4:11	2:39	2:54	4:34	5:07	5:03	3:17	3:43	5:35	6:41	4:29	4:27	3:50	4:01	3:41	1:47	4:18	4:56	2:48	1:48	11:00	2:19	4:00	4:28
Ayr			5:28	4:28	8:11	6:42	6:31	7:10	2:24	5:43	5:25	4:41	8:32	1:48	7:54	3:03	0:48	6:11	7:48	5:56	3:51	7:24	3:10	5:06	4:32	5:55	5:22	4:29	4:16	3:56	3:28	7:34	5:29	6:34	9:37	1:53	8:31	7:49	7:13	7:37	4:57	5:23	7:40	7:37	4:43	7:46	6:12	5:50	4:22	7:16
Birmingham				2:15	3:04	1:41	1:43	2:09	3:16	0:36	1:01	1:40	3:25	5:12	2:53	7:05	4:45	1:10	3:01	2:59	7:31	2:37	2:32	2:21	2:05	1:01	1:55	1:49	1:46	2:55	3:28	2:46	1:08	1:27	4:36	5:33	3:30	2:42	2:06	2:39	1:36	0:59	2:33	2:39	1:02	2:44	9:52	0:49	2:21	2:11
Bradford					4:30	3:34	2:43	4:03	2:17	2:19	1:34	0:53	4:37	4:17	4:46	6:06	3:46	3:03	4:01	2:49	6:31	3:37	1:32	1:18	0:28	2:02	1:35	1:22	0:57	1:32	2:06	3:46	1:37	3:05	6:29	4:33	5:24	4:20	3:44	4:18	1:00	2:15	4:12	3:50	1:36	4:38	8:52	2:42	0:59	3:32
Brighton						2:49	2:09	3:26	6:00	2:42	3:15	3:53	1:53	7:53	3:41	9:49	7:29	2:47	2:19	5:39	10:14	2:20	5:15	4:35	4:19	2:57	3:43	4:32	4:29	5:08	5:42	3:05	3:21	1:58	5:24	8:16	4:18	1:14	1:39	1:54	3:49	3:45	1:35	1:41	3:45	4:01	12:35	3:07	4:35	1:27
Bristol							3:02	0:56	4:31	1:44	2:21	2:59	3:18	6:27	1:37	8:20	6:00	0:47	3:27	4:13	8:45	3:28	3:46	3:41	3:25	2:17	3:11	3:03	3:01	4:15	4:48	3:58	2:28	1:30	3:20	6:48	2:14	2:03	1:26	1:37	2:56	2:14	1:54	2:58	2:17	1:30	11:07	1:07	3:41	2:07
Cambridge								3:28	4:20	1:30	1:52	2:03	2:06	6:04	4:11	8:09	5:49	2:29	1:28	4:20	8:35	1:04	3:56	2:37	2:34	1:25	1:47	3:12	3:10	3:19	3:52	1:13	1:41	1:55	5:54	6:37	4:49	2:34	1:51	2:47	2:15	2:26	2:35	1:19	2:26	4:03	10:56	2:08	2:45	1:17
Cardiff									4:58	2:15	2:48	3:27	3:54	6:54	2:02	8:47	6:27	1:16	4:03	4:23	9:13	4:03	4:14	4:09	3:53	2:46	3:39	3:31	3:28	4:42	5:16	4:31	2:55	2:05	3:46	7:15	2:40	2:38	2:01	2:12	3:23	2:24	2:29	3:33	2:44	0:53	11:34	1:35	4:09	2:43
Carlisle										3:30	3:12	2:28	6:19	2:08	5:41	4:01	1:41	3:58	5:35	3:44	4:27	5:11	0:58	2:54	2:19	3:43	3:10	2:16	2:04	1:44	1:15	5:21	3:17	4:21	7:25	2:29	6:19	5:36	5:00	5:24	2:45	3:10	5:28	5:25	2:31	5:34	6:48	3:38	2:10	5:07
Coventry											1:03	1:41	3:05	5:29	2:55	7:22	5:02	1:12	2:49	3:13	7:48	2:21	2:49	2:23	2:06	0:45	1:39	2:06	2:03	2:56	3:30	2:31	1:09	1:04	4:38	5:50	3:32	2:19	1:43	2:17	1:37	1:18	2:11	2:20	1:19	2:49	10:09	0:56	2:22	1:53
Derby												0:57	3:33	4:58	3:31	7:02	4:42	1:48	3:09	2:52	7:27	2:45	2:28	1:39	1:23	0:49	1:24	1:45	1:42	2:13	2:46	2:55	0:33	1:51	5:14	5:29	4:08	3:06	2:30	3:04	0:54	1:21	2:58	2:48	0:53	3:22	9:49	1:27	1:39	2:19
Doncaster													3:58	4:13	4:12	6:19	3:59	2:30	3:21	3:17	6:44	2:57	2:16	0:56	0:43	1:27	0:55	1:48	1:25	1:28	2:02	3:07	1:02	2:30	5:56	4:46	4:50	3:45	3:09	3:43	0:30	2:13	3:36	3:11	1:44	4:04	9:05	2:09	0:54	2:57
Dover														7:56	4:14	10:08	7:48	3:16	2:16	5:59	10:34	2:17	5:35	4:29	4:26	3:14	3:40	4:52	4:49	5:11	5:45	3:02	3:34	2:27	5:57	8:36	4:51	2:23	2:08	2:50	4:06	4:05	2:38	1:37	4:05	4:29	12:55	3:36	4:38	1:34
Edinburgh															7:38	3:01	1:05	5:55	7:20	5:41	3:02	6:56	2:55	4:38	4:04	5:26	4:54	4:13	4:00	3:00	2:23	7:06	5:01	6:18	9:21	1:02	8:16	7:33	6:57	7:21	4:29	5:07	7:25	7:09	4:28	7:30	5:24	5:34	3:54	6:57
Exeter																9:31	7:11	1:58	4:36	5:24	9:56	4:37	4:57	4:52	4:36	3:28	4:22	4:14	4:12	5:26	5:59	5:07	3:39	2:46	1:54	7:59	0:53	2:38	2:43	1:55	4:07	3:25	2:27	4:02	3:28	2:37	12:18	2:18	4:52	3:16
Fort William																	2:26	7:49	9:26	7:35	1:32	9:02	4:49	6:44	6:10	7:34	7:00	6:07	5:54	5:34	5:06	9:12	7:07	8:12	11:15	2:09	10:10	9:27	8:51	9:15	6:35	7:01	9:19	9:16	6:22	9:24	4:04	7:28	6:01	8:56
Glasgow																		5:28	7:05	5:13	3:08	6:41	2:28	4:23	3:49	5:12	4:39	3:46	3:33	3:13	2:45	6:51	4:46	5:51	8:54	1:10	7:48	7:06	6:30	6:54	4:14	4:40	6:57	6:55	4:01	7:03	5:29	5:07	3:40	6:36
Gloucester																			3:25	3:42	8:14	3:22	3:15	3:10	2:54	1:46	2:39	2:32	2:29	3:43	4:17	3:31	1:56	1:11	3:39	6:16	2:33	2:00	1:24	1:42	2:24	1:42	1:52	2:56	1:45	1:49	10:35	0:36	3:10	2:05
Harwich																				5:38	9:53	0:42	5:13	3:55	3:52	2:43	3:05	4:30	4:28	4:37	5:10	1:32	2:59	2:26	6:20	7:55	5:14	2:49	2:17	3:12	3:33	3:44	3:01	1:09	3:44	4:38	12:14	3:26	4:03	1:42
Holyhead																					7:58	5:16	2:59	3:39	2:49	3:23	3:52	1:53	2:13	3:53	4:26	5:25	3:15	4:06	7:06	6:00	6:00	5:21	4:45	5:05	3:06	2:10	5:12	5:18	2:11	4:33	10:19	3:19	3:19	4:47
Inverness																						9:27	5:14	7:10	6:35	7:59	7:26	6:32	6:20	5:41	5:04	9:37	7:33	8:37	11:41	2:10	10:35	9:52	9:16	9:40	7:01	7:26	9:44	9:41	6:47	9:50	2:31	7:54	6:26	9:21
Ipswich																							4:50	3:31	3:28	2:20	2:41	4:06	4:04	4:13	4:46	1:08	2:35	2:27	6:21	7:31	5:15	2:50	2:18	3:13	3:09	3:20	3:02	1:10	3:20	4:39	11:50	3:02	3:39	1:43
Kendal																								2:44	1:53	3:02	3:00	1:36	1:23	1:38	1:59	5:00	2:54	3:41	6:44	3:13	5:38	4:56	4:20	4:44	2:22	2:30	4:47	4:53	1:50	4:53	7:32	2:57	2:04	4:22
Kingston upon Hull																									1:08	2:08	0:58	2:13	1:49	1:54	2:27	3:18	1:43	3:10	6:36	5:12	5:30	4:25	3:49	4:23	1:11	2:53	4:17	3:43	2:25	4:44	9:31	2:49	1:02	3:39
Leeds																										1:53	1:25	1:23	0:58	1:20	1:53	3:37	1:27	2:55	6:21	4:38	5:15	4:10	3:34	4:08	0:50	2:16	4:02	3:40	1:37	4:29	8:57	2:34	0:46	3:23
Leicester																											1:16	2:17	2:14	2:42	3:15	2:27	0:46	1:32	5:11	6:01	4:05	2:47	2:11	2:45	1:23	1:43	2:39	2:29	1:24	3:20	10:20	1:25	2:08	2:01
Lincoln																												2:31	2:02	2:11	2:44	2:20	0:59	2:28	6:07	5:29	5:01	3:43	3:07	3:41	1:07	2:33	3:34	2:54	2:10	4:16	9:48	2:21	1:35	2:51
Liverpool																													0:48	2:28	3:01	4:16	2:10	2:56	6:00	4:33	4:54	4:11	3:35	3:59	1:52	1:25	4:03	4:09	1:06	3:48	8:53	2:13	1:54	3:39
Manchester																														2:03	2:36	4:12	1:51	2:52	5:55	4:22	4:49	4:07	3:30	3:55	1:14	1:41	3:58	4:04	1:01	4:04	8:41	2:08	1:29	3:37
Middlesbrough																															0:55	4:20	2:15	3:43	7:09	3:40	6:03	4:58	4:22	4:56	1:43	3:20	4:50	4:24	2:40	5:17	8:02	3:22	1:05	4:12
Newcastle upon Tyne																																4:54	2:49	4:17	7:43	3:03	6:37	5:32	4:56	5:30	2:17	3:54	5:24	4:58	3:14	5:51	7:25	3:56	1:43	4:46
Norwich																																	2:44	2:58	6:51	7:40	5:45	3:31	2:48	3:43	3:18	3:29	3:32	2:00	3:28	5:06	11:59	3:10	3:48	2:13
Nottingham																																		1:57	5:23	5:34	4:17	3:12	2:36	3:10	0:57	1:44	3:04	2:49	1:18	3:31	9:53	1:36	1:42	2:25
Oxford																																			4:30	6:40	3:24	1:28	0:45	1:25	2:25	2:08	1:19	1:56	2:09	2:40	10:59	1:31	3:10	1:15
Penzance																																				9:43	1:41	4:22	4:27	3:39	5:51	5:09	4:11	5:46	5:12	4:20	14:02	4:02	6:36	4:59
Perth																																					8:37	7:54	7:18	7:42	5:03	5:28	7:46	7:43	4:49	7:52	4:30	5:55	4:28	7:24
Plymouth																																						3:16	3:20	2:32	4:44	4:02	3:04	4:39	4:05	3:14	12:55	2:55	5:29	3:54
Portsmouth																																							1:18	0:52	3:39	3:23	0:32	2:11	3:23	3:13	12:13	2:20	4:25	1:39
Reading																																								1:22	3:01	2:45	1:09	1:46	2:45	2:37	11:35	1:44	3:47	0:56
Salisbury																																									3:37	3:09	0:40	2:37	3:12	2:47	12:02	2:02	4:22	1:52
Sheffield																																										2:08	3:32	3:22	1:40	3:59	9:22	2:04	1:11	2:53
Shrewsbury																																											3:16	3:22	1:04	2:45	9:46	1:23	2:46	2:53
Southampton																																												2:26	3:15	3:05	12:05	2:12	4:16	1:40
Southend-on-Sea																																													3:21	4:09	12:02	3:03	3:51	1:07
Stoke-on-Trent																																														3:18	9:08	1:23	2:09	2:53
Swansea																																															12:11	2:10	4:44	3:18
Thurso																																																10:15	8:47	11:43
Worcester																																																	2:49	2:24
York																																																		3:39

Distance in miles

	Aberdeen	Aberystwyth	Ayr	Birmingham	Bradford	Brighton	Bristol	Cambridge	Cardiff	Carlisle	Coventry	Derby	Doncaster	Dover	Edinburgh	Exeter	Fort William	Glasgow	Gloucester	Harwich	Holyhead	Inverness	Ipswich	Kendal	Kingston upon Hull	Leeds	Leicester	Lincoln	Liverpool	Manchester	Middlesbrough	Newcastle upon Tyne	Norwich	Nottingham	Oxford	Penzance	Perth	Plymouth	Portsmouth	Reading	Salisbury	Sheffield	Shrewsbury	Southampton	Southend-on-Sea	Stoke-on-Trent	Swansea	Thurso	Worcester	York
Aberystwyth	471
Ayr	181	324
Birmingham	423	114	272
Bradford	377	159	196	124
Brighton	596	258	441	169	263
Bristol	505	122	375	88	215	129
Cambridge	487	198	366	102	156	117	167
Cardiff	525	106	377	106	233	168	42	201
Carlisle	229	232	89	183	107	345	286	256	288
Coventry	442	134	297	18	124	157	102	84	129	200
Derby	418	137	269	41	88	188	134	99	159	180	43
Doncaster	371	192	239	95	40	232	184	117	210	150	94	57
Dover	620	315	477	195	284	81	194	118	233	393	180	208	244
Edinburgh	126	340	75	284	198	466	377	326	379	91	303	266	212	444
Exeter	581	199	425	161	282	170	75	323	107	336	166	213	257	244	439
Fort William	159	430	136	391	305	568	478	456	486	198	415	387	345	591	131	549
Glasgow	146	322	36	291	203	468	378	355	384	96	313	282	245	491	46	449	100
Gloucester	473	109	317	53	171	152	35	132	53	228	59	93	149	189	331	107	435	324
Harwich	568	258	411	170	224	130	203	64	234	323	152	167	185	129	397	262	524	419	171
Holyhead	452	96	315	151	158	330	204	252	209	226	167	156	169	358	316	279	423	323	189	331
Inverness	105	492	198	449	353	620	536	490	558	260	458	421	369	601	157	607	63	162	496	554	481
Ipswich	538	268	420	156	210	125	206	54	240	311	138	155	171	127	381	264	510	409	177	21	307	538
Kendal	280	182	139	151	62	324	235	215	232	50	170	136	99	344	141	307	248	146	200	279	180	310	268
Kingston upon Hull	398	235	255	139	68	243	228	134	239	165	123	94	37	254	230	290	367	255	195	204	218	387	189	127
Leeds	359	171	198	119	9	256	209	144	226	111	117	74	32	275	190	279	309	208	167	217	162	345	197	72	60
Leicester	445	155	294	43	99	163	118	70	140	214	24	30	73	183	282	189	412	312	83	146	182	431	125	166	98	97
Lincoln	411	208	249	87	80	207	170	88	192	178	76	53	41	206	247	241	376	274	135	152	204	402	124	140	46	72	52
Liverpool	354	120	199	99	67	267	180	179	169	110	113	90	89	294	201	240	308	213	142	265	95	370	236	75	126	73	110	118
Manchester	349	128	204	87	37	252	167	159	188	117	99	58	51	273	208	239	315	215	132	230	120	363	211	72	96	42	95	87	34
Middlesbrough	289	233	181	174	69	316	265	196	287	92	175	130	84	316	147	337	279	192	230	266	226	306	253	77	88	64	154	127	134	106
Newcastle upon Tyne	252	266	146	209	98	345	300	232	312	58	209	165	115	350	104	369	237	153	263	297	257	263	287	88	130	96	188	153	167	136	40
Norwich	536	270	348	163	185	174	234	62	256	280	142	146	142	169	351	284	478	378	193	72	289	505	44	249	145	178	112	103	222	177	221	252
Nottingham	416	155	267	54	78	191	140	84	165	188	52	15	48	210	256	218	386	286	108	165	177	410	140	141	92	72	27	37	107	68	128	159	118
Oxford	497	151	335	68	167	106	73	92	106	267	57	101	138	142	358	151	465	365	47	134	208	515	128	223	175	162	76	123	168	157	218	253	159	104
Penzance	688	301	552	269	394	279	184	343	218	463	278	316	369	355	551	109	663	561	217	374	388	715	375	419	412	391	310	359	353	344	449	481	393	323	261
Perth	86	366	85	336	245	509	412	370	422	134	346	309	254	485	43	487	103	59	362	439	360	113	424	184	273	233	326	290	244	254	191	148	394	299	404	598
Plymouth	619	232	461	203	325	206	111	274	159	372	209	254	300	286	485	43	592	490	150	305	322	648	305	348	326	323	231	284	299	281	379	412	327	255	193	75	529
Portsmouth	579	231	440	147	274	50	95	132	138	357	132	184	231	137	448	127	555	455	114	161	303	603	158	308	268	245	166	209	254	237	315	360	200	191	83	235	486	170
Reading	538	180	399	103	213	79	77	90	112	309	90	138	184	115	402	141	506	406	75	129	264	554	126	263	209	207	113	168	193	197	264	295	152	129	25	251	445	184	60
Salisbury	538	178	383	121	245	82	53	140	101	312	113	159	207	158	400	91	510	408	73	177	262	569	177	265	251	230	132	187	213	208	287	318	200	162	65	201	443	132	43	57
Sheffield	390	173	235	79	40	225	163	121	193	154	75	35	21	268	230	245	352	250	139	185	164	387	176	102	66	33	68	46	74	40	102	133	144	37	137	361	273	293	228	160	203
Shrewsbury	419	73	260	47	100	216	116	140	107	171	64	67	114	249	262	175	369	267	77	215	104	424	195	125	163	102	79	123	59	67	166	203	196	86	105	286	309	218	195	147	150	85
Southampton	564	213	401	128	235	64	75	129	122	330	114	167	201	150	433	106	528	426	98	157	287	590	162	276	249	230	136	189	235	215	288	320	190	162	66	217	476	149	20	47	23	206	175
Southend-on-Sea	549	258	431	152	220	85	177	64	211	342	129	168	185	89	395	226	548	438	152	57	303	549	57	283	200	213	139	156	255	225	262	299	99	160	105	337	439	269	117	98	132	197	173	126
Stoke-on-Trent	381	108	243	47	75	217	127	137	140	150	64	36	74	236	241	202	348	248	95	201	122	410	179	121	117	78	55	87	56	36	142	173	171	55	118	311	287	241	201	147	168	50	35	183	199
Swansea	529	76	368	124	220	209	80	236	41	279	150	184	244	264	370	154	477	375	91	279	172	578	279	249	262	229	174	226	168	187	293	323	286	178	144	266	446	196	175	147	136	202	124	159	245	159
Thurso	212	584	304	557	461	728	644	589	640	352	552	529	475	706	262	715	169	268	604	657	589	108	654	402	492	453	544	510	463	471	410	367	613	519	621	823	220	758	709	662	664	506	523	682	659	502	631
Worcester	448	96	309	29	135	162	62	119	73	220	46	68	124	197	306	136	418	311	28	168	151	480	174	169	166	146	72	118	108	101	203	229	180	85	57	244	350	177	146	95	101	103	49	124	150	65	97	572
York	345	193	201	129	34	269	227	151	237	116	129	84	33	269	187	289	314	214	181	232	185	344	200	81	38	24	108	76	96	65	48	83	176	84	174	400	230	331	257	217	244	54	132	244	214	114	268	450	164
London	537	228	440	118	203	53	118	61	151	309	97	129	171	76	403	179	511	404	116	86	277	562	82	263	214	195	103	155	211	209	251	283	117	128	59	285	451	216	84	41	92	166	161	82	43	161	187	669	136	211

Scale to Map Pages 4-169

1:158,400 = 2.5 miles to 1 inch (2.54 cm) / 1.6 km to 1 cm

0 1 2 3 4 5 10 15 20 Miles

0 1 2 3 4 5 10 15 20 25 30 Kilometres

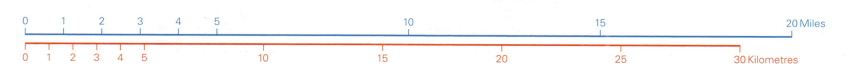

Motorway	M1
Autoroute	
Autobahn	

Motorway Under Construction
Autoroute en construction
Autobahn im Bau

Motorway Proposed
Autoroute prévue
Geplante Autobahn

Motorway Junctions with Numbers
Unlimited Interchange 4
Limited Interchange 5

Autoroute échangeur numéroté
Echangeur complet
Echangeur partiel

Autobahnanschlußstelle mit Nummer
Unbeschränkter Fahrtrichtungswechsel
Beschränkter Fahrtrichtungswechsel

Motorway Service Area (with fuel station)
with access from one carriageway only

Aire de services d'autoroute (avec station service)
accessible d'un seul côté
Rastplatz oder Raststätte (mit tankstelle)
Einbahn

Major Road Service Area (with fuel station) with 24 hour facilities
Primary Route   Class A Road
Aire de services sur route prioritaire (avec station service) Ouverte 24h sur 24
Route à grande circulation   Route de type A
Raststätte (mit tankstelle) Durchgehend geöffnet
Hauptverkehrsstraße   A- Straße

Major Road Junctions   Detailed
Jonctions grands routiers   Détaillé
Hauptverkehrsstraße Kreuzungen   Ausführlich
   Other Autre Andere

Truckstop (selection of)
Sélection d'aire pour poids lourds
Auswahl von Fernfahrerrastplatz

Primary Route   A41
Route à grande circulation
Hauptverkehrsstraße

Primary Route Junction with Number   5
Echangeur numéroté
Hauptverkehrsstraßenkreuzung mit Nummer

Primary Route Destination   DOVER
Route prioritaire, direction
Hauptverkehrsstraße Richtung

Dual Carriageways (A & B roads)
Route à double chaussées séparées (route A & B)
Zweispurige Schnellstraße (A- und B- Straßen)

Class A Road   A129
Route de type A
A-Straße

Class B Road   B177
Route de type B
B-Straße

Narrow Major Road (passing places)
Route prioritaire étroite (possibilité de dépassement)
Schmale Hauptverkehrsstraße (mit Überholmöglichkeit)

Major Roads Under Construction
Route prioritaire en construction
Hauptverkehrsstraße im Bau

Major Roads Proposed
Route prioritaire prévue
Geplante Hauptverkehrsstraße

Safety Cameras with Speed Limits
Single Camera   30
Multiple Cameras located along road   50
Single & Multiple Variable Speed Cameras   V V
Radars de contrôle de vitesse
Radar simple
Radars multiples situés le long de la route
Radars simples et multiples de contrôle de vitesse variable
Sicherheitskameras mit Tempolimit
Einzelne Kamera
Mehrere Kameras entlang der Straße
Einzelne und mehrere Kameras für variables Tempolimit

Fuel Station
Station service
Tankstelle

Gradient 1:7 (14%) & steeper
(descent in direction of arrow)
Pente égale ou supérieure à 14% (dans le sens de la descente)
14% Steigung und steiler (in Pfeilrichtung)

Toll   Toll
Barrière de péage
Gebührenpflichtig

Dart Charge
www.gov.uk/pay-dartford-crossing-charge

Park & Ride   P+R
Parking avec Service Navette
Parken und Reisen

Mileage between markers   8
Distence en miles entre les flèches
Strecke zwischen Markierungen in Meilen

Airport
Aéroport
Flughafen

Airfield
Terrain d'aviation
Flugplatz

Heliport   H
Héliport
Hubschrauberlandeplatz

Ferry   Bac   Fähre
(vehicular, sea)   (véhicules, mer)   (auto, meer)
(vehicular, river)   (véhicules, rivière)   (auto, fluß)
(foot only)   (piétons)   (nur für Personen)

Railway and Station
Voie ferrée et gare
Eisenbahnlinie und Bahnhof

Level Crossing and Tunnel
Passage à niveau et tunnel
Bahnübergang und Tunnel

River or Canal
Rivière ou canal
Fluß oder Kanal

County or Unitary Authority Boundary
Limite de comté ou de division administrative
Grafschafts- oder Verwaltungsbezirksgrenze

National Boundary
Frontière nationale
Landesgrenze

Built-up Area
Agglomération
Geschloßene Ortschaft

Town, Village or Hamlet
Ville, Village ou hameau
Stadt, Dorf oder Weiler

Wooded Area
Zone boisée
Waldgebiet

Spot Height in Feet   · 813
Altitude (en pieds)
Höhe in Fuß

Relief above 400' (122m)
Relief par estompage au-dessus de 400' (122m)
Reliefschattierung über 400' (122m)

National Grid Reference (kilometres)   ¹00
Coordonnées géographiques nationales (Kilomètres)
Nationale geographische Koordinaten (Kilometer)

Page Continuation   48
Suite à la page indiquée
Seitenfortsetzung

Area covered by Main Route map   MAIN ROUTE 180
Repartition des cartes des principaux axes routiers
Von Karten mit Hauptverkehrsstrecken

Area covered by Town Plan   PAGE 194
Ville ayant un plan à la page indiquée
Von Karten mit Stadtplänen erfaßter Bereich

Abbey, Church, Friary, Priory   †
Abbaye, église, monastère, prieuré
Abtei, Kirche, Mönchskloster, Kloster

Animal Collection
Ménagerie
Tiersammlung

Aquarium
Aquarium
Aquarium

Arboretum, Botanical Garden
Jardin Botanique
Botanischer Garten

Aviary, Bird Garden
Volière
Voliere

Battle Site and Date   1066
Champ de bataille et date
Schlachtfeld und Datum

Blue Flag Beach
Plage Pavillon Bleu
Blaue Flagge Strand

Bridge
Pont
Brücke

Butterfly Farm
Ferme aux Papillons
Schmetterlingsfarm

Castle (open to public)
Château (ouvert au public)
Schloß / Burg (für die Öffentlichkeit zugänglich)

Castle with Garden (open to public)
Château avec parc (ouvert au public)
Schloß mit Garten (für die Öffentlichkeit zugänglich)

Cathedral   ✝
Cathédrale
Kathedrale

Cidermaker
Cidrerie (fabrication)
Apfelwein Hersteller

Country Park
Parc régional
Landschaftspark

Distillery
Distillerie
Brennerei

Farm Park, Open Farm
Park Animalier
Bauernhof Park

Fortress, Hill Fort
Château Fort
Festung

Garden (open to public)
Jardin (ouvert au public)
Garten (für die Öffentlichkeit zugänglich)

Golf Course
Terrain de golf
Golfplatz

Historic Building (open to public)
Monument historique (ouvert au public)
Historisches Gebäude (für die Öffentlichkeit zugänglich)

Historic Building with Garden (open to public)
Monument historique avec jardin (ouvert au public)
Historisches Gebäude mit Garten (für die Öffentlichkeit zugänglich)

Horse Racecourse
Hippodrome
Pferderennbahn

Industrial Monument
Monument Industrielle
Industriedenkmal

Leisure Park, Leisure Pool
Parc d'Attraction, Loisirs Piscine
Freizeitpark, Freizeit pool

Lighthouse
Phare
Leuchtturm

Mine, Cave
Mine, Grotte
Bergwerk, Höhle

Monument
Monument
Denkmal

Motor Racing Circuit
Circuit Automobile
Automobilrennbahn

Museum, Art Gallery   M
Musée
Museum, Galerie

National Park
Parc national
Nationalpark

National Trail
Sentier national
Nationaler Weg

National Trust Property
National Trust Property
National Trust- Eigentum

Natural Attraction   ★
Attraction Naturelle
Natürliche Anziehung

Nature Reserve or Bird Sanctuary
Réserve naturelle botanique ou ornithologique
Natur- oder Vogelschutzgebiet

Nature Trail or Forest Walk
Chemin forestier, piste verte
Naturpfad oder Waldweg

Picnic Site
Lieu pour pique-nique
Picknickplatz

Place of Interest   Craft Centre •
Site, curiosité
Sehenswürdigkeit

Prehistoric Monument
Monument Préhistorique
Prähistorische Denkmal

Railway, Steam or Narrow Gauge
Chemin de fer, à vapeur ou voie étroite
Eisenbahn, Dampf- oder Schmalspurbahn

Roman Remains
Vestiges Romains
Römischen Ruinen

Theme Park
Centre de loisirs
Vergnügungspark

Tourist Information Centre   i
Office de Tourisme
Touristinformationen

Viewpoint   (360 degrees)   (180 degrees)
Vue panoramique   (360 degrés)   (180 degrés)
Aussichtspunkt   (360 Grade)   (180 Grade)

Vineyard
Vignoble
Weinberg

Visitor Information Centre   V
Centre d'information touristique
Besucherzentrum

Wildlife Park
Réserve de faune
Wildpark

Windmill
Moulin à vent
Windmühle

Zoo or Safari Park
Parc ou réserve zoologique
Zoo oder Safari-Park

The Skerries
(Ynysoedd y Moelrhoniaid)

Carmel Head
(Trwyn y Gader)

Middle Mouse
(Ynys Badrig)

West Mouse
(Maen y Bugael)

Porth
Wen

East Mouse
(Ynys Amlwch)

Cemaes
Bay

Bull Bay
(Porthllechog)

Bull Bay (Porth Llechog)

Cemlyn
Bay

Penrhyn

Wylfa

Tregele

Cemaes

A5025

Burwen

Amlwch
Port

Llaneilian

Amlwch

B5111

Pengorffwysfa

Llanfairynghornwy

Thomas
Mon

Llanbadrig

Llanfechell

Bodewryd

Carreglefn

Rhosgoch

Penysarn

Parys
Mountain

Gadfa

Nebo

Llanddeusant

Mynydd
Mechell

Rhosybol

A5025

Penygraigwen

City Dulas

Llan

Church Bay
(Porth Swtan)

Swtan

Rhydwyn

Llanrhyddlad

Llanfflewyn

Llyn
Llygeirian

Llanbabo

Llyn Alaw

Gwredog

Brynr

Llandyfrydog

Ari

HOLYHEAD BAY
(BAE CAERGYBI)

Llanfaethlu

A5025

Llanfwrog

Llanddeusant

Llynnon

Melin
Hywel

Llyn Alaw

Llanerchymedd

Bachau

Magnaddwyn

Llanerchymedd
Station

B5112

Carmel

Capel
Coch

Holyhead to:
Dublin 3hrs. 15mins.
Dublin 1hr. 50mins.
(Fast Ferry)

Breakwater

Gogarth
Bay

Caer Y
Twr Hillfort

Porth-y-
felin

Salt Island

HOLYHEAD
(Caergybi)

Tregwehelydd
Standing Stone

Pen-llyn

ANGLESEY

(YNYS MÔN)

Tryfil

Ellins Tower

Llaingoch

Fort

Arch

Llanfachraeth

Llanynghenedl

Presaddfed Burial
Chambers

Trefor

Rhosmei

Holyhead Mountain
Hut Circles

HOLY

Stryd

Penrhos

Trefignath

Newlands
Park

B5109

Llangwyllog

Llynfaes

Cefni Resr

Holyhead
Feilw
Standing Stones

Kingsland

Porth
Dafarch
Ancient Huts

Ty Mawr
Standing Stone

Valley
(Y Fali)

Bodedern

A5

Oriel Ynys Môn

Rhosmeirc

Trearddur

ISLAND

YNYS GYBI

Four Mile
Bridge

B4545

A55

3

Caergeiliog

2

4

A5

Bryngwran

B5109

ANGLESEY

Mona

Bodffordd

Heneglwys

Rhostrenwfa

Llangefni

Llyn
Penrhyn

Llanfihangel
yn Nhowyn

6

A5

Llyn Dinam

Llanfairy-
neubwll

Llyn Traffwll

Capel
Gwyn

5

Dotham

Cerrigceinwen

Gwalchmai

Pentre Berw

St Gwenfaen's
Well

RAF
Valley

Ty Newydd
Burial Chamber

A4080

Pencarnisiog

Soar

Bethel

Trefdraeth

Capel
Mawr

Din Dryfol
Chambered Tomb

B4422

A55

6

Cymyran
Bay

Bryn Du

Afon Cefni

Malltraeth Marsh
(Cors Ddyga)

B4419

Rhosneigr

Llanfaelog

Llyn
Maelog

Llangadwaladr

Llyn
Coron

Malltraeth

Llangaffo

Bodowyr Burial
Chamber

Barclodiad Y
Gawres Grave

Hermion

A4080

Castell
Bryn Gwyn

Llangwyfan-isaf

Aberffraw

Bodorgan

B4421

Lacia Talo

Anglesey

St Cwyfan's
'The Church in the Sea'

Aberffraw
Bay

Malltraeth Sands

Newborough
(Niwbwrch)

Dwyran

B4419

Anglesey
Model Village

Foel Farm
Park

**Malltraeth
Bay**

Newborough
Forest

Abermenai
Point

Llanddwyn Island
(Ynys Llanddwyn)

Llanddwyn
Bay

Llanfaglan

Foryd
Bay

Caernarfon
Bay

Saron

CAERNARFON BAY

(BAE CAERNARFON)

Airworld

Dinas Dinlle

Llandwrog

Glynllifon

Inigo Jones
Slate Works

A499

Penygroes

Pontllyfni

Llanllyfni

Aberdesach

Clynnog-fawr

Capel
Uchaf

Tai'n Lon

A487

St Beuno

St Beuno's
Well 1671

Pant Glas

Trefor

Bwlch Mawr

Gyrn Ddu

Bwlchderwin

Trwyn y
Gorlech

Yr Eifl

Tre'r Ceiri

Gym Ddu
1712

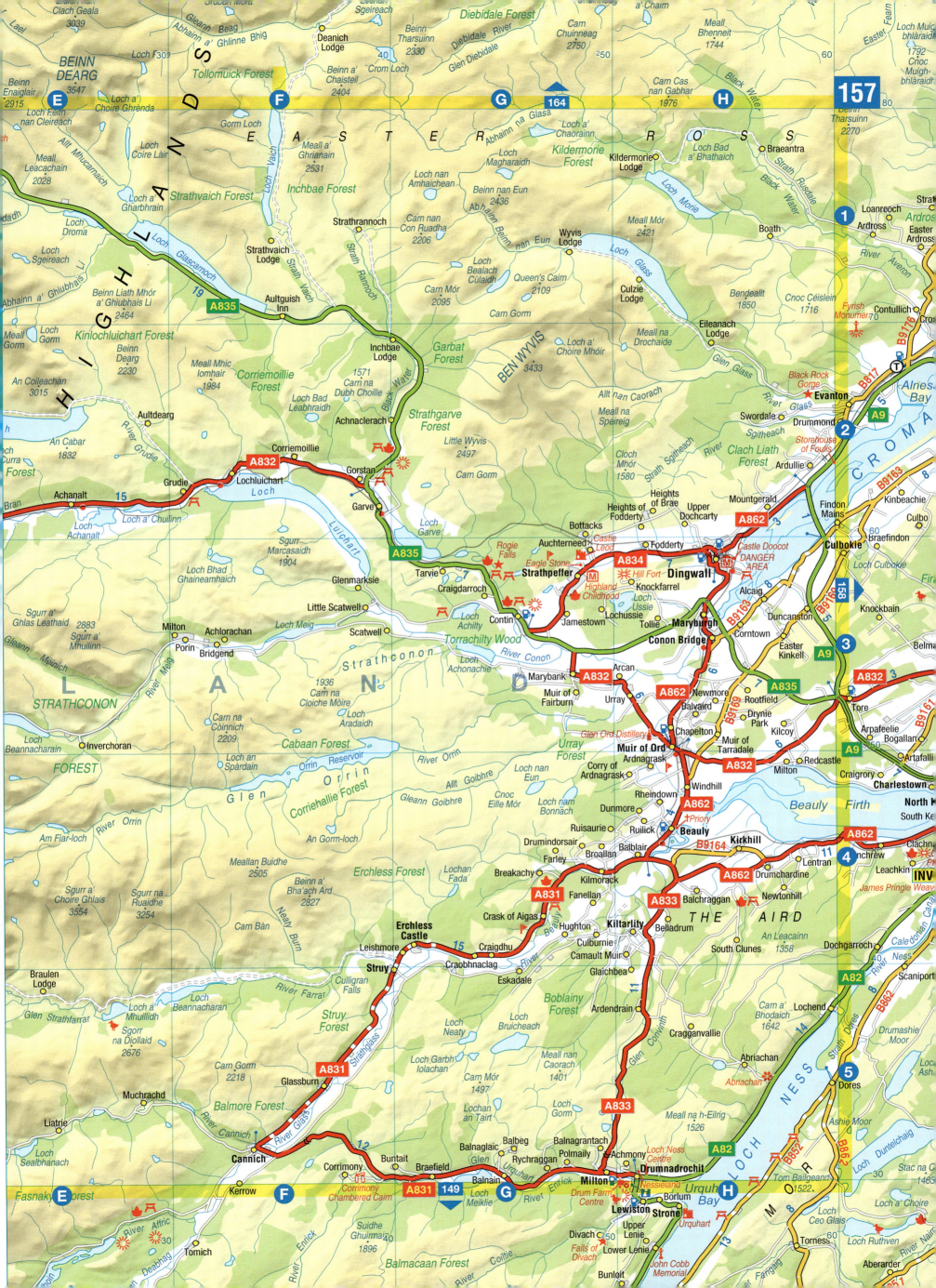

162

30
60 · · 70 · · 80 · · 90 ·

A · · · B · · · C · · · D

1

20

2

10

◄ 171

3

900

4

90

5

80
60 · · 70 · · · · · 90 ·

A · · · 155 · · · B · · · C **A832** · · · D

Camas Eilean
Ghlais

Reiff

Eilean
Mullagrach

Isle Ristol

Glas-leac
Mór

Tanera Beg

Summer

Ullapool to
Stornoway 2hrs. 40mins.

Glas-leac
Beag

Eilean Dubh

Priest Island

Bottle
Island

Greenstone
Point

Rubha
Beag

Loch na
Doire Duinne

Opinan

Mellon
Udrigle

Gruinard
Island

Stattic
Point

Loch nan
Clachan
Geala

Loch a'
Choire

Eilean Furadh
Mór

Slaggan Bay

Loch an
t-Slagain

Beinn
Dearg Nhór
513

Achgarve

Mungasdale

Rubha
Reidh

Camas
Mór

Loch an
Draing

Cove

Rubha
nan
Sasan

Mellon
Charles

Laide

Gruinard
Bay

Gruinard
House

An Cuaidh
972

Loch Airigh
an Eilein

Mellangaun

Ormiscaig

Aultbea

A832

Second
Coast

B8057

Isle of Ewe

Drumchork

First
Coast

Loch
na Bà

Beinn Dearg
Bad Chailleach
897

Melvaig

Aultgrishan

B8021

Loch
Sguod

Midtown

Brae

Loch Ewe

Loch a'
Bhaid-
luachraich

Loch
Fada

Seana Chamas

Cnoc Breac
962

Loch
Mhic' ille
Riabhaich

Loch na
Mòine Buige

Aird
Dubh

Beinn a'
Chàisgein
Beag
2230

Peterburn

Naast

Inverewe

Meall
na Mèine
·820

Bad
Bog

Port Erradale

North
Erradale

Loch
nan
Liagh

Loch Bad a'
Chreamh

River Sand

Loch na
Curra

Londubh

Poolewe

River Ewe

Loch
Ghiuragarstidh

Loch na
Moine

Lochan
Beannach Mór

B8021

Big Sand

Caolas Beag

Lonemore

Mial

Strath

Heritage
M

5

A832

Loch
Tollaidh

Tollie
Farm

Loch
Kernsary

Longa
Island

Smithstown

Gairloch

Loch Gairloch

Eilean

Loch Airigh
a' Phuill

Meall an
Doirein
·1381

2595
Beinn
Airigh Charr

eisiadar